I0134264

UNNECESSARY TATTOO
&
Other Stains on a
Stainless Steel Heart

poems by

John L. Holgerson

Finishing Line Press
Georgetown, Kentucky

UNNECESSARY TATTOO

&

Other Stains on a
Stainless Steel Heart

ACKNOWLEDGMENTS

I am indebted to N.K. Wagner, the editor of the online literary journal, *Page
& Spine*, for her unwavering faith in my work. Five of the poems in this book
found their home in her magazine.

"High White Stone House" and "Unnecessary Tattoo" first appeared in *Page
& Spine*, the July 19, 2013 edition

"On the Exhumation of Neftali Ricardo Reyes Basoalto" "The Alibi" and
"Spy" first appeared in *Page & Spine*, the July 11, 2014 edition

"Dead Roses" first appeared on the web site *The Vincent van Gogh Gallery* (www.
vggallery.com) February 20, 2013

Editor: Christen Kincaid

Cover Art: John L. Holgerson

Author Photo: John L. Holgerson

Printed in the USA on acid-free paper.
Order online: www.finishinglinepress.com
also available on amazon.com

Author inquiries and mail orders:
Finishing Line Press
P. O. Box 1626
Georgetown, Kentucky 40324
U. S. A.

Table of Contents

*The poems we write are merely tattoos
we have peeled from the skin of our hearts*

High White Stone House

I don't think of you much
in this high white stone house
with silence an unseen shade
drawn on each unshuttered window

Outside, the buzz of flies on poppies
as loud as saws on redwood
The clop of hooves on carved rock stairs
as empty as the chairs in the living room

No sound replicates your laughter
burning moussaka in the kitchenette
or your violin serenading the gypsies
on the boats in the horseshoe harbor

The creak of the door
creeps across these walls
The breath of the wind stutters

You standing on the terrace
naked from the back
a ghost who sometimes mutters

When shutters close at day's end
a hungry dark slides over me
inside this high white stone house
this hollow unending echo of you

Dead Roses

I cannot write a poem

the way you painted a portrait.

I cannot write a line

the way you drew one.

But Vincent

I have been in that

second floor room

with the two chairs

one against the wall

one next to the bed

and leaned out

the only window

at first light

wondering

if by

painting them

you were

trying

to save

the roses

dying on the

outdoor tables

of the night café

across the street.

Lies

Of the thousand nights alone
when I was supposed
to be with you
the ones that break the heart
are the ones when it was
supposed to be true

Spy

She caught you
peering
through the keyhole of her heart

You didn't see the
fighting
such espionage could start

Her coded messages
concealing
how much hung by a nail

The broken cipher
revealing
the details of your betrayal

It isn't easy
trading
secrets you don't own

nor is it easy
learning
love is out on loan

The Alibi

I am the alibi
for your random indiscretions
for your cell phone shut offs
for your missed appointments

I am the alibi
who will not break
when the authorities ask
if I know your whereabouts

on the nights
you slipped by
the sleeping sentries
of the hapless heart

when they subtly hint
at torture yet to come
the unlicensed dentist
the machinist manicurist

the heavy set man
of Mediterranean descent
with the smell of talc
and gunpowder on his palms

Crown of thorns
on my head
stake of holly
through my heart

I will not talk
for I am the alibi
who wants
to be the crime

On the Exhumation of Neftali Ricardo Reyes Basoalto

Classical musicians played cellos and guitars
outside the rickety cemetery gate
Spade diggers stabbed the hardscrabble earth

Was it the carcinoma creep inside his prostate
or the toxic seep from an assassin's needle
that divorced him from the seduced muse

who aroused him to write the fevered line
"Carnal apple, woman filled, burning moon"

The Chilean government issued a passport
for sections of a dead man's desiccated skeleton
to be distilled in a sterile North Carolina lab

Finding no trace of manmade poison nor
any more poetic marrow to be sucked out
onto the pages left blank in his last journal

perhaps they took some lingering DNA molecule
from a cracked shard of decaying bone
isolated the sweeping sequence of nucleotides

that engorged the genome the muse stroked
to allow Neftali Ricardo Reyes Basoalto
to discharge images in lead and ink from a heaving heart

revealing
the carnal apple's bitter sweetness
the filled woman's utter emptiness
the burning moon's polar loneliness

Author's note: Neftali Ricardo Reyes Basoalto is the birth name for the Chilean poet Pablo Neruda

The Gypsy Woman Tells All

The moon was an azure mote
amid the astral shrapnel in God's eye
when the man entered the gypsy woman's
house on a warm evening in July.

They sat at the kitchen table
in a yellow jukebox glow
the stones, the cards, the ball
lined up like judges in a row.

"Gypsy, roll the runes at midnight
across the empty graves
of the self-proclaimed atheists
whose souls have all been saved."

"I see the churches and chapels
where you knelt to plead
your prayers unanswered
your wounds not grieved.

Between the coin and the toss
between the gold and the dross
between the nails and the Cross
Faith demands a cost."

"Nimbly turn the tarot. Show me
The Fool, a smile on his face
lying next to the naked woman
pouring water from her vase."

"I see the frames for the photographs
that you never took
of the memories you can't find now
no matter where you look.

Between the moth and the flame
between the bullet and the brain
between the praise and the blame
Hope whispers your name."

"Then read the love line in my palm
so broken, so incomplete;
touch the blistered intersection
where yours and mine might meet."

"I see the box of letters
that you never sent
I hear the words you spoke
that you never meant.

Between the sleeve and the heart
between the song and the lark
between the donkey and the cart
Desire must ignite the spark."

When he left the gypsy's house
it was a cold night in July.
The moon still an azure mote
amid the astral shrapnel in God's eye.

There is a war

There is a war
between the rhymed and the unrhymed
between the structured and the unstructured
between the metaphor chained by sound
and the dangling simile

I did not know there was this war

I was writing in a cross-fire
oblivious to the wounds inflicted
by the rubber bullet ballads
hollowed out and packed
with the sharp slivers of rhyme
yanked from fingertips
following the orders of the ancients
unaware of their syntactic treason

I did not know there was this war

Captured by the granite guerillas
of modern poetry gone wild
those rebels
                    revolting against rhyme
stabbing the eyes
                    with the sharp shrapnel
of misplaced broken sentences

I did not know there was this war

Shackled with poetic conventions
I was taken to a court
without a judge
                given a racket
made to play tennis
                without a net
against an old man shouting

"I will not quit;
nor will I submit!"

as he pounded tennis balls
in perfect metric beats

until the beady-eyed guardians
of Versa Libra advanced on us
their javelins filled with red ink
to haul him away by his heels
his head bouncing on the clay

Then this hog butcher hobo
from the land of Lincoln
places his hand upon my shoulder
and with rutabaga on his chin
mumbles with regret

"I really didn't think
the leopard would eat the zebra."

The End of Days

Poets are liars who tell the truth
—*Jean Cocteau*

When the computer scientists and politicians
came for the last of the poets and playwrights
they found them hiding amid the stacks in the
only library left standing after the digital coup

Armed with electrolyzed Nooks and Kindles
they prodded the scribblers to the town square
where soldiers carrying joysticks with hundred
round ammo clips saluted and executed them

With their writings shrouds of tender tinder
the technocrats anointed them with the sacred oil
lit their stacked bodies with leaking lithium chips
holding hands and singing songs to elevator music

As the ash of allegory, alliteration, metaphor and flesh
ascended into the indifferent cobalt-coated sky
the beep, buzz, hum and chirp of iPhones and iPads
filled the carbon-toxic air in auto-tonal celebration

Free

I never thought I'd feel this free
from guilt and sin and apathy.

I never thought I'd feel this sane
with nothing left for me to gain.

You rolled away the stone, unlocked the chain
broke the seal on the heart so it could love again.

I never thought I'd feel this free
from games and lies and hypocrisy.

I never thought I'd feel this calm
while holding nothing in my palm.

You rolled away the stone, unlocked the chain
broke the seal on the heart so it could love again.

You rolled away the stone, tore off the chain
broke the seal on the heart so it could love again.

The Road to Vlychos

In the morning,
the road we walked to Vlychos
is a hot, twisting snake
of pavement, rocks and dirt.

Sun worshippers line the sides
of the ancient ever-rising path.
Cats with uncared for heavy coats

(all cats along the road to Vlychos
are strays)

lie among the tall wild weeds
beneath the sea-facing hills
while ageless women lie nude

(all women along the road to Vlychos
are either nudes or strays)

on large multi-colored towels
out on the gravel ledge
where once we did the same.

There is no scarcity of views or ghosts
along the curving road to Vlychos.

Book of Desire

I hear you want to erase
the chapters you can't forget
Dissolve our past embraces
in the acrid acid of false regret.

I know you wish you'd never shared
the sacred secrets that you did
the ones that made us cry
the ones you kept so well hid

among the texts on your cell phone
and the pictures that you sent
to those whom you admired
who paid your beauty testament.

It doesn't matter how often
you hit the worried word "delete"
our history has been etched on
the hard drive of time by human heat.

So put your hand in mine now
I'll accept any apology that's sweet
and we can write new chapters
in a book that never was complete.

Ubiquity

I thought I could write
just one damn poem
without thinking of you

See one yellow flower
along the uneven road's edge
and not think of your hair

See one bluebird fluttering
in the budding lemon trees
and not think of your eyes

Late morning light melts
the last stubborn shadows
warms the placid Aegean
and diminishes the stars

You are asleep beneath
the same constant constellations
five thousand miles from me

You are here

Unnecessary Tattoo

A bruised heart cleaved in two
stitched down the middle
No mystery or enigma here
no obscure or secret riddle

It's there behind your eyes
It's the catch in your voice
at the mention of star-crossed lovers
or the vagaries of choice

It can be seen in the ashes
of the cigarettes you snuff out
the lingering sparks of memory
in your holy grail of doubt

Don't tell me when it's done
the needle round and thin
the short hot veneer of pain
the stain upon the skin

It's just another private part
you'll likely hide from view
a duplicitous reminder
an unnecessary tattoo

John L. Holgerson is the author of *Broken Borders*, a collection of poems (Wasteland Press, 2012). His work has appeared in small literary journals such as *Modern English Tanka*, *Shadow Quill Poetry*, and in online literary magazines such as *Page & Spine* as well as at the Vincent van Gogh Gallery (www.vggallery.com). He has been a featured poet at various poetry venues in Massachusetts and is listed in *Poets & Writers'* Directory of Poets and Writers (www.pw.org/content/john_holgerson). For three decades, he was a trial and appellate attorney with the Massachusetts public defender office. He now practices law with a small law firm in Taunton, Massachusetts where he lives. His author's web site is www.johnlholgerson.com.